Welcome to the Pink Rush Business Journal. This Journal will help you get and stay organized. Rather you're an aspiring boss or experienced this Journal will motivate you to stay on track to be successful.

This Pink Rush Business Journal Belongs to:

_____

_____

_____

❝

I want to grow. I want to be better. You Grow. We all grow. We're made to grow.You either evolve or you disappear.

Tupac Shakur

Pink Rush Business Journal

First Printing
ISBN - 978-1-943284-56-6
A2Z Books Publishing Lithonia, GA 30058
www.A2ZBooksPublishing.net
Manufactured in the United States of America
A2Z Books Publishing has allowed this work to remain
exactly as the Publisher & Author Intended

Pink Rush

Business Options :

- Hair Business
- Lip Gloss Business
- Tshirt Business
- Apparel Business
- Skincare Business
- Lash Business
- Nail Business
- Cotton Candy Business
- Cookie Business
- Author/Book Business
- Candy Maker
- Inventor
- Illustrator
- Baker
- Jewelry Designer
- _____ (write your own)
- _____ (write your own)
- _____ (write your own)

Things you Need to Start a
Business

- ☐ Business Name Product/Service
- ☐ Website
- ☐ Location for Business (Online or Brick & Mortar)
- ☐ Business Bank Account
- ☐ EIN
- ☐ Merchant Service
- ☐ LLC (Business Registration)
- ☐ Business Licenses/Selling Permits
- ☐ Other (write what applies to you)

_____

_____

Why Do you want to Start a Business Questionnaire

Write 10 reasons you want to Start a Business:

1. _____

2. _____

3. _____

4. _____

5. _____

6. _____

7. _____

8. _____

9. _____

10. _____

" Successful entrepreneurs are givers and not takers of positive energy.

Anonymous

MONTHLY *Schedule*

Month of _____

WEEK 1 _____

_____

_____

_____

_____

WEEK 2 _____

_____

_____

_____

_____

WEEK 3 _____

_____

_____

_____

_____

WEEK 4 _____

_____

_____

_____

_____

MONTHLY *To-Do List*

Month of _____

MONDAY _____

_____

_____

TUESDAY _____

_____

_____

WEDNESDAY _____

_____

_____

THURSDAY _____

_____

_____

FRIDAY _____

_____

_____

SATURDAY _____

_____

_____

SUNDAY _____

_____

_____

MONTHLY *Goals*

Month of _____

GOAL 1	GOAL 2	GOAL 3

ACTION STEPS	☑	ACTION STEPS	☑	ACTION STEPS	☑

DEADLINE:	DEADLINE:	DEADLINE:

Pink Rush Business Promotion Tip:

Use every opportunity you can to promote your business!

MONTHLY
Business Reflection

1. What Obstacles and Fears do I have about starting my Business?

_____

_____

_____

_____

_____

2. What can I do to overcome these Fears and Obstacles?

_____

_____

_____

_____

_____

3. Who and what can help me to overcome these obstacles?

_____

_____

_____

_____

_____

I Will Have a Successful Business!

ReWrite & Site

TOP
Business Notes

_____
_____
_____
_____
_____
_____
_____
_____
_____
_____
_____
_____
_____
_____
_____
_____
_____
_____

All business is personal...

Make your friends before you need them.

Robert Louis Johnson

MONTHLY *Schedule*

Month of _____

WEEK 1 _____

_____

_____

_____

_____

WEEK 2 _____

_____

_____

_____

_____

WEEK 3 _____

_____

_____

_____

_____

WEEK 4 _____

_____

_____

_____

_____

MONTHLY *To-Do List*

Month of _____

MONDAY _____

_____

_____

TUESDAY _____

_____

_____

WEDNESDAY _____

_____

_____

THURSDAY _____

_____

_____

FRIDAY _____

_____

_____

SATURDAY _____

_____

_____

SUNDAY _____

_____

_____

MONTHLY *Goals*

Month of _____

GOAL 1	GOAL 2	GOAL 3

ACTION STEPS	☑	*ACTION STEPS*	☑	*ACTION STEPS*	☑

DEADLINE:	*DEADLINE:*	*DEADLINE:*

Pink Rush Business Promotion Tip:

Make sure your website is clean, professional, and always up to date.

MONTHLY
Business Reflection

1. What Obstacles and Fears do I have about starting my Business?

_____

_____

_____

_____

_____

2. What can I do to overcome these Fears and Obstacles?

_____

_____

_____

_____

_____

3. Who and what can help me to overcome these obstacles?

_____

_____

_____

_____

_____

I Will Have a Successful Business!

ReWrite & Site

TOP
Business Notes

_____
_____
_____
_____
_____
_____
_____
_____
_____
_____
_____
_____
_____
_____
_____
_____
_____
_____

The Moment You Give Up
is the Moment You Let
Someone Else Win.

Kobe Bryant

MONTHLY *Schedule*

Month of _____

WEEK 1 _____

_____

_____

_____

_____

WEEK 2 _____

_____

_____

_____

_____

WEEK 3 _____

_____

_____

_____

_____

WEEK 4 _____

_____

_____

_____

_____

MONTHLY *To-Do List*

Month of _____

MONDAY _____

_____

_____

TUESDAY _____

_____

_____

WEDNESDAY _____

_____

_____

THURSDAY _____

_____

_____

FRIDAY _____

_____

_____

SATURDAY _____

_____

_____

SUNDAY _____

_____

_____

MONTHLY *Goals*

Month of _____

GOAL 1	GOAL 2	GOAL 3

ACTION STEPS	☑	ACTION STEPS	☑	ACTION STEPS	☑

DEADLINE:	DEADLINE:	DEADLINE:

Pink Rush Business Promotion Tip:

*Always make sure
you are selling
the right product.*

MONTHLY
Business Reflection

1. What Obstacles and Fears do I have about starting my Business?

_____

_____

_____

_____

_____

2. What can I do to overcome these Fears and Obstacles?

_____

_____

_____

_____

_____

3. Who and what can help me to overcome these obstacles?

_____

_____

_____

_____

_____

I Will Have a Successful Business!

ReWrite & Site

TOP
Business Notes

_____
_____
_____
_____
_____
_____
_____
_____
_____
_____
_____
_____
_____
_____
_____
_____
_____
_____
_____
_____
_____

"

Don't settle for average

Bring your best to the moment.

**Then, whether it fails or succeeds,
at least you know you gave all you had.
We need to live the best that's in us.**

Angela Bassett

MONTHLY *Schedule*

Month of _____

WEEK 1
_____

_____

_____

_____

_____

WEEK 2
_____

_____

_____

_____

_____

WEEK 3
_____

_____

_____

_____

_____

WEEK 4
_____

_____

_____

_____

_____

MONTHLY *To-Do List*

Month of _____

MONDAY _____

_____

_____

TUESDAY _____

_____

_____

WEDNESDAY _____

_____

_____

THURSDAY _____

_____

_____

FRIDAY _____

_____

_____

SATURDAY _____

_____

_____

SUNDAY _____

_____

_____

MONTHLY *Goals*

Month of _____

GOAL 1	GOAL 2	GOAL 3

ACTION STEPS	☑	ACTION STEPS	☑	ACTION STEPS	☑

DEADLINE:	DEADLINE:	DEADLINE:

Pink Rush Business Promotion Tip:

Make sure you understand your target market.

MONTHLY
Business Reflection

1. What Obstacles and Fears do I have about starting my Business?

_____
_____
_____
_____
_____

2. What can I do to overcome these Fears and Obstacles?

_____
_____
_____
_____
_____

3. Who and what can help me to overcome these obstacles?

_____
_____
_____
_____
_____

I Will Have a Successful Business!

ReWrite & Site

TOP
Business Notes

_____

_____

_____

_____

_____

_____

_____

_____

_____

_____

_____

_____

_____

_____

_____

_____

_____

_____

You Just Can't Beat the Person

Who Never Gives Up.

Babe Ruth

MONTHLY *Schedule*

Month of _____

WEEK 1 _____

_____

_____

_____

_____

WEEK 2 _____

_____

_____

_____

_____

WEEK 3 _____

_____

_____

_____

_____

WEEK 4 _____

_____

_____

_____

_____

MONTHLY *To-Do List*

Month of _____

MONDAY _____

_____

_____

TUESDAY _____

_____

_____

WEDNESDAY _____

_____

_____

THURSDAY _____

_____

_____

FRIDAY _____

_____

_____

SATURDAY _____

_____

_____

SUNDAY _____

_____

_____

MONTHLY *Goals*

Month of _____

GOAL 1	GOAL 2	GOAL 3

ACTION STEPS	☑	ACTION STEPS	☑	ACTION STEPS	☑

DEADLINE: DEADLINE: DEADLINE:

Pink Rush Business Promotion Tip:

Use visual media to build your social media presence.

MONTHLY
Business Reflection

1. What Obstacles and Fears do I have about starting my Business?

_____

_____

_____

_____

_____

2. What can I do to overcome these Fears and Obstacles?

_____

_____

_____

_____

_____

3. Who and what can help me to overcome these obstacles?

_____

_____

_____

_____

_____

I Will Have a Successful Business!

ReWrite & Site

TOP
Business Notes

_____
_____
_____
_____
_____
_____
_____
_____
_____
_____
_____
_____
_____
_____
_____
_____
_____
_____
_____
_____

Business opportunities are like buses

there's always another one coming.

Richard Branson

MONTHLY *Schedule*

Month of _____

WEEK 1 _____

_____
_____
_____
_____
_____

WEEK 2 _____

_____
_____
_____
_____
_____

WEEK 3 _____

_____
_____
_____
_____
_____

WEEK 4 _____

_____
_____
_____
_____
_____

MONTHLY *To-Do List*

Month of _____

MONDAY _____

_____

_____

TUESDAY _____

_____

_____

WEDNESDAY _____

_____

_____

THURSDAY _____

_____

_____

FRIDAY _____

_____

_____

SATURDAY _____

_____

_____

SUNDAY _____

_____

_____

MONTHLY *Goals*

Month of _____

GOAL 1	GOAL 2	GOAL 3

ACTION STEPS	☑	ACTION STEPS	☑	ACTION STEPS	☑

DEADLINE:	DEADLINE:	DEADLINE:

Pink Rush Business Promotion Tip:

Have your customers share your product on their social media accounts

MONTHLY
Business Reflection

1. What Obstacles and Fears do I have about starting my Business?

_____

_____

_____

_____

_____

2. What can I do to overcome these Fears and Obstacles?

_____

_____

_____

_____

_____

3. Who and what can help me to overcome these obstacles?

_____

_____

_____

_____

_____

I Will Have a Successful Business!

ReWrite & Site

TOP
Business Notes

_____

_____

_____

_____

_____

_____

_____

_____

_____

_____

_____

_____

_____

_____

_____

_____

_____

_____

_____

_____

"

Passion is Energy.

Feel the power that comes from focusing on what excites you

Oprah Winfrey

MONTHLY *Schedule*

Month of _____

WEEK 1 _____

_____
_____
_____
_____

WEEK 2 _____

_____
_____
_____
_____

WEEK 3 _____

_____
_____
_____
_____

WEEK 4 _____

_____
_____
_____
_____

MONTHLY *To-Do List*

Month of _____

MONDAY _____

_____

_____

TUESDAY _____

_____

_____

WEDNESDAY _____

_____

_____

THURSDAY _____

_____

_____

FRIDAY _____

_____

_____

SATURDAY _____

_____

_____

SUNDAY _____

_____

_____

MONTHLY *Goals*

Month of _____

GOAL 1	GOAL 2	GOAL 3

ACTION STEPS	☑	*ACTION STEPS*	☑	*ACTION STEPS*	☑

DEADLINE: **DEADLINE:**   **DEADLINE:**

Pink Rush Business Promotion Tip:

Make Sure Your Promotion is Better than the Competition

MONTHLY
Business Reflection

1. What Obstacles and Fears do I have about starting my Business?

_____

_____

_____

_____

_____

2. What can I do to overcome these Fears and Obstacles?

_____

_____

_____

_____

_____

3. Who and what can help me to overcome these obstacles?

_____

_____

_____

_____

_____

I Will Have a Successful Business!

ReWrite & Site

TOP
Business Notes

_____
_____
_____
_____
_____
_____
_____
_____
_____
_____
_____
_____
_____
_____
_____
_____
_____
_____
_____

If you really look closely,

most overnight successes took a long time

Steve Jobs

MONTHLY *Schedule*

Month of _____

WEEK 1 _____

_____
_____
_____
_____
_____

WEEK 2 _____

_____
_____
_____
_____
_____

WEEK 3 _____

_____
_____
_____
_____
_____

WEEK 4 _____

_____
_____
_____
_____
_____

MONTHLY *To-Do List*

Month of _____

MONDAY _____

_____

_____

TUESDAY _____

_____

_____

WEDNESDAY _____

_____

_____

THURSDAY _____

_____

_____

FRIDAY _____

_____

_____

SATURDAY _____

_____

_____

SUNDAY _____

_____

_____

MONTHLY *Goals*

Month of _____

GOAL 1	GOAL 2	GOAL 3

ACTION STEPS	☑	ACTION STEPS	☑	ACTION STEPS	☑

DEADLINE: DEADLINE: DEADLINE:

Pink Rush Business Promotion Tip:

Make sure you have an email list of past customers.

MONTHLY
Business Reflection

1. What Obstacles and Fears do I have about starting my Busi-

_____

_____

_____

_____

_____

2. What can I do to overcome these Fears and Obstacles?

_____

_____

_____

_____

_____

3. Who and what can help me to overcome these obstacles?

_____

_____

_____

_____

_____

I Will Have a Successful Business!

ReWrite & Site

TOP
Business Notes

Even if you are on the right track, you'll get run over if you just sit there.

Will Rodgers

MONTHLY *Schedule*

Month of _____

WEEK 1 _____

_____

_____

_____

_____

_____

WEEK 2 _____

_____

_____

_____

_____

_____

WEEK 3 _____

_____

_____

_____

_____

_____

WEEK 4 _____

_____

_____

_____

_____

_____

MONTHLY *To-Do List*

Month of _____

MONDAY _____

_____

_____

TUESDAY _____

_____

_____

WEDNESDAY _____

_____

_____

THURSDAY _____

_____

_____

FRIDAY _____

_____

_____

SATURDAY _____

_____

_____

SUNDAY _____

_____

_____

MONTHLY *Goals*

Month of _____

GOAL 1	GOAL 2	GOAL 3

ACTION STEPS	☑	*ACTION STEPS*	☑	*ACTION STEPS*	☑

DEADLINE: *DEADLINE:*   *DEADLINE:*

Pink Rush Business Promotion Tip:

Collaborate with other business owners.

MONTHLY
Business Reflection

1. What Obstacles and Fears do I have about starting my Busi-

_____

_____

_____

_____

_____

2. What can I do to overcome these Fears and Obstacles?

_____

_____

_____

_____

_____

3. Who and what can help me to overcome these obstacles?

_____

_____

_____

_____

_____

I Will Have a Successful Business!

ReWrite & Site

TOP
Business Notes

_____
_____
_____
_____
_____
_____
_____
_____
_____
_____
_____
_____
_____
_____
_____
_____
_____
_____
_____

> # *Don't be afraid to give up*
> ## the good to go for the great

John D. Rockefeller

MONTHLY *Schedule*

Month of _____

WEEK 1 _____

_____
_____
_____
_____
_____

WEEK 2 _____

_____
_____
_____
_____
_____

WEEK 3 _____

_____
_____
_____
_____
_____

WEEK 4 _____

_____
_____
_____
_____
_____

MONTHLY *To-Do List*

Month of _____

MONDAY _____

_____

_____

TUESDAY _____

_____

_____

WEDNESDAY _____

_____

_____

THURSDAY _____

_____

_____

FRIDAY _____

_____

_____

SATURDAY _____

_____

_____

SUNDAY _____

_____

_____

MONTHLY *Goals*

Month of _____

GOAL 1	GOAL 2	GOAL 3

ACTION STEPS	☑	ACTION STEPS	☑	ACTION STEPS	☑

DEADLINE: DEADLINE: DEADLINE:

Pink Rush Business Promotion Tip:

Make sure your product are priced properly.

MONTHLY
Business Reflection

1. What Obstacles and Fears do I have about starting my Busi-

_____

_____

_____

_____

_____

2. What can I do to overcome these Fears and Obstacles?

_____

_____

_____

_____

_____

3. Who and what can help me to overcome these obstacles?

_____

_____

_____

_____

_____

I Will Have a Successful Business!

ReWrite & Site

TOP
Business Notes

_____
_____
_____
_____
_____
_____
_____
_____
_____
_____
_____
_____
_____
_____
_____
_____
_____
_____
_____
_____
_____

If everything was perfect,

you would never learn and you would never grow.

Beyonce Knowles

MONTHLY *Schedule*

Month of _____

WEEK 1 _____

_____

_____

_____

_____

_____

WEEK 2 _____

_____

_____

_____

_____

_____

WEEK 3 _____

_____

_____

_____

_____

_____

WEEK 4 _____

_____

_____

_____

_____

_____

MONTHLY *To-Do List*

Month of _____

MONDAY _____

_____

_____

TUESDAY _____

_____

_____

WEDNESDAY _____

_____

_____

THURSDAY _____

_____

_____

FRIDAY _____

_____

_____

SATURDAY _____

_____

_____

SUNDAY _____

_____

_____

MONTHLY *Goals*

Month of _____

GOAL 1	GOAL 2	GOAL 3

ACTION STEPS	☑	ACTION STEPS	☑	ACTION STEPS	☑

DEADLINE:	DEADLINE:	DEADLINE:

Pink Rush Business Promotion Tip:

Make sure you are using wor of mouth marketing.

MONTHLY
Business Reflection

1. What Obstacles and Fears do I have about starting my Busi-

_____

_____

_____

_____

_____

2. What can I do to overcome these Fears and Obstacles?

_____

_____

_____

_____

_____

3. Who and what can help me to overcome these obstacles?

_____

_____

_____

_____

_____

I Will Have a Successful Business!

ReWrite & Site

TOP
Business Notes

_____

_____

_____

_____

_____

_____

_____

_____

_____

_____

_____

_____

_____

_____

_____

_____

_____

_____

ORDER FORM: DATE:

Client Name:

Contact Number:

Shipping Method: Shipping Costs:

Tracking #:   Date Shipped:

Order Details:

Subtotal: Notes:

Tax:

Discount:

Total:

ORDER FORM: DATE:

Client Name:

Contact Number:

Shipping Method: Shipping Costs:

Tracking #:   Date Shipped:

Order Details:

Subtotal: Notes:

Tax:

Discount:

Total:

ORDER FORM: DATE:

Client Name:

Contact Number:

Shipping Method: Shipping Costs:

Tracking #:   Date Shipped:

Order Details:

Subtotal: Notes:

Tax:

Discount:

Total:

ORDER FORM: DATE:

Client Name:

Contact Number:

Shipping Method: Shipping Costs:

Tracking #:   Date Shipped:

Order Details:

Subtotal:

Tax:

Discount:

Total:

Notes:

ORDER FORM: DATE:

Client Name:

Contact Number:

Shipping Method: Shipping Costs:

Tracking #:   Date Shipped:

Order Details:

Subtotal: Notes:

Tax:

Discount:

Total:

ORDER FORM:

DATE:

Client Name:

Contact Number:

Shipping Method:

Shipping Costs:

Tracking #:

Date Shipped:

Order Details:

Subtotal:

Tax:

Discount:

Total:

Notes:

ORDER FORM: **DATE:**

Client Name:

Contact Number:

Shipping Method: Shipping Costs:

Tracking #:   Date Shipped:

Order Details:

Subtotal: Notes:

Tax:

Discount:

Total:

ORDER FORM: **DATE:**

Client Name:

Contact Number:

Shipping Method: Shipping Costs:

Tracking #:   Date Shipped:

Order Details:

Subtotal: Notes:

Tax:

Discount:

Total:

ORDER FORM:

DATE:

Client Name:

Contact Number:

Shipping Method:

Shipping Costs:

Tracking #:

Date Shipped:

Order Details:

Subtotal:

Notes:

Tax:

Discount:

Total:

ORDER FORM: DATE:

Client Name:

Contact Number:

Shipping Method: Shipping Costs:

Tracking #:   Date Shipped:

Order Details:

Subtotal: Notes:

Tax:

Discount:

Total:

Interested in Writing and/or Publishing a Book?
Visit **www.a2zbookspublishing.net**